Cultural Diplomacy

About the Author

Leilani Tamu is a poet, historian and former New Zealand diplomat. Born in Aotearoa-New Zealand in 1982, her ancestry connects her to the islands of Samoa and Tonga. In 2013 Tamu was the Fulbright-Creative New Zealand Pacific Writer in residence at the University of Hawai'i (Mānoa). In 2014 she published her debut poetry collection *The Art of Excavation* (Anahera Press). Tamu currently lives in Auckland, New Zealand.

Acknowledgement is made to the editors of *Landfall* and *School Journal* in which some of the poems in this book first appeared.

First published 2017

Leilani Tamu
Auckland
New Zealand
www.leilanitamu.com

© 2017 Leilani Tamu

ISBN 978-0-473-41713-0

Thanks to Fulbright and Creative New Zealand for providing the author with the opportunity to develop work for this collection by sponsoring a three month residency at the University of Hawai'i (Mānoa).

Special thanks to Siobhan Harvey, Kiri Piahana-Wong and Paula Green for providing support and advice during the manuscript development process.

This book is copyright. Apart from fair dealing for the purpose of private study, research, criticism or review, as permitted under the Copyright Act, no part may be reproduced by any process without the prior permission of the author. All enquiries should be directed to Leilani.Tamu@gmail.com in the first instance.

for
my beloved
Leafaitulagi
8 July 1930 – 11 July 2017

Contents

1	SOS	i
2	Whero is Red	5
3	Tuahine	17
4	Lobotomy	27
5	Broken Waters	47
6	Day Break	61

SOS

White Poppy

White Poppy
I am searching for you
in a sea of red.

Researching Aliʻi

I searched for you in boxes
    the archivist muttered *poison*

I searched for you in texts
    the librarian whispered *incest*

I searched for you in images
    the cashier demanded *money*

I found you in mele
    the people chant *aloha*

Ka'iulani

They suffocated you with pity
after staging an illegal coup.

They photographed you with envy
after staging an illegal coup.

They mourned you with glee
after staging an illegal coup.

They market you with greed
honouring an illegal coup.

An Exchange

First time, blood and fear.
Second time, maybe better.
Diary note: close shop.

Whero is Red

1982: Senryu

First love, then marriage
a High Mass, baby carriage…
tote-ticket divorce.

Lullaby Love

Hush little baby, hush: don't say a word
dive into that dream, hold onto maybe
maybe he forgot the mocking bird.
Hush little baby, hush.

Dry your tears, little lady
forget what you've heard
bury the past, opt for crazy

hope, no matter how listless, how absurd
was the secret gift, he tucked away safely
in your cot, undisturbed.
Hush little baby, hush.

My Sister and I

We were TAB kids
    my sister and I
horses flew
    unicorn-like
on the racecourse
when Dad's bets were *up*.

We were KFC kids
    my sister and I
chicks cried
    child-like
in the car park
when Dad's chips were *down*.

We were Sky Tower kids
    my sister and I
women flocked
    geese-like
to the casino
when Dad's luck *won*.

We were Rugby League kids
    my sister and I
men fought
    warrior-like
on the field
when Dad's team *lost*.

We were TAB kids
    we were KFC kids
we were Sky Tower kids
    we were Rugby League kids
my sister and I
when Dad
    was *alive*.

Stepfather No.1

I was eight
when you left   us
for another woman
with two kids.

You told me to sit

on the floor
eat with the dog   wait
for your return
wait   for years.

Stepfather No.2

I was broken when I first saw your face
little-girl-veteran, who'd lost the wooden-spoon-war
too angry and bitter to love you then, in any case

it was easier to love strange boys on the chase
than risk another man breaking my heart's law
I was broken, when I first saw your face

never realized why He gave me the middle name Grace
till it was too late, too raw, too sore
too angry and bitter to love you then, in any case

easier to disappear without a trace
jumped out the window, forgot the door
I was broken, when I first saw your face

had no idea, didn't care, about sense of place
on the street, there is only one law
too angry and bitter to love you then, in any case

but perhaps that was the point of my efface
to break my core and lose the war in the search for more
I was broken, when I first saw your face
too angry and bitter to love you then, in any case

Hangi Pants

My Aunt said everyone knew
there was a hāngī cooking
behind the library

a fishy secret
hooked in the mouths
of Foodtown girls
in love
with whitebait.

Behind the library
books anchored me
to the ground

as the boys
lined up
two-by-two.

Maths 101

Lesson 1:
Mr Lorenz said I would be wasting my time
    sitting School C. Maths

    on the same day

Mrs Gude said I should consider getting tested
    for STDs

Lesson 2:
I crunched the numbers
    calculated the odds

    made the call

took the test
    passed   the exam

His Story

In His Story girls like us
shut our mouths
close our legs
hold on tight
until he says so.

In His Story girls like us
open our mouths
spread our legs
come on down
when he says so.

In His Story girls like us
tell lies
lie down
bend over
if he says so.

In His Story girls like us
aren't important
get paid less
shut up
because he says so.

Writing Back

again you type-cast her
into a role of your design

in telling 'her story' you validate
your own imported perceptions

of time, place and 'race'
Oh Imperial Gaze

the one who never means
to create that kind of terrible

Oppression

you put Narcissus
to shame

Tuahine

Tuahine

you kiss the tips of the Koʻolau
with such tender longing

I can't help but desire
your touch

Midnight in Mānoa

last night a moʻo whispered in my ear
as I slept in the sacred heart
of the Koʻolau

soft whispers fell
in liquid notes
on my lashes

leaving me
drenched in a stream
of midnight
meaning

Telesā
for Lani Wendt Young

Lani, with your pen
you ignite ancient fires
spark rage; fan embers
pour lava in open mouths
flood forbidden canyons
rip open celestial arteries
and then gently
pierce the heart
of Pulotu, with love

Diasporic Dreams
written in collaboration with David Keali'i MacKenzie

wrapped in your love, woven memories
arrive on the back of the fourth wind
each word a tender parcel
carefully folded into notes
melodious aloha

you call out to a distant shore
where your child waits
your love the anchor
your soul the guide

songs plaited through ukulele, guitar, refrain
a calm rocking of your moʻopuna
an unfurled gift to carry them
across the currents and remind them
of all the meanings
for home

you call out to a distant shore
where your child waits
your love the anchor
your soul the guide

wrapped in your love, woven memories
call me back, call me home
to the islands of your heart
to the gentle strum
of your guitar

Fatu

Old Honu came to see me today
at Tagaloa's behest
he journeyed
from the Sacred
South to Hawaiki
to pay tribute
to the baby
swimming
in my lagoon

O‘ahu

in Waimanalo I found your na‘au
tucked into the black-singed
crevices of the Ko‘olau

there I planted a kiss
on your red lips
a small offering

for the baby
for Hawaiki
for the tears

feeding the life
within

Subversion
for every "Nameless" Samoan Woman

Special Collections: Day 1 –

He has plastered your face on to the front of His book
not even bothered to tell me your name
Subtext: to him you are *nothing*

I want to rip you out.

Special Collections: Day 2 –

He has plastered your breasts on to the front of His book
not even bothered to tell me your name
Subtext: to him you are *nothing*

I want to rip you out
give you back to your 'aiga.

Special Collections: Day 3 –

He has plastered your butt on to the front of His book
not even bothered to tell me your name

I want to rip you out
give you back to your 'aiga
Subtext: to them you are *everything.*

Lobotomy

Tripping Nafanua-style

yes this is a Nafanua poem
I've been dreaming
dreaming about her
jumping ship
taking a trip
going nuts
on the
strip

   oh oh what's going on? Something's up with this Nafanua poem, I mean
      she's the heroine right? not the one who got it wrong, but somehow I
           missed a beat, cause in my dreams she's a sex machine

go go go
trussed up vision
got to write this crazy
poem pull finger reclaim
night woman of fame awash
with shame in the midst of churlish
cries condemn   refrain   and reclaim your name

Lobotomy
for Janet Frame

Would they still love you if he'd carried out the lobotomy?
Small incisions mask deep wounds.

Would they still love you if he'd carried out the lobotomy?
Deep wounds mask small incisions.

Would they still love you if he'd carried out the lobotomy?
Small wounds mask deep incisions.

Mansfield

I have to admit I never cared much for you
privilege turns me *off*

And then your lover's chess set landed on my desk
passion turns me *on*

Strange, naked, ivory woman
you thumb through pages of *scandal*

Are you safely locked up in your dollhouse?
for you are, after all, *delicious*

Left Out
for Robyn Hyde

I was with you
when you tore off
your clothes   jumped
into the sea's embrace

conceived an idea
fertilized by Auckland-muck
too radical to be your own
too radical to be Left   alone

girls like us
are connected
by salt, blood
and water

Alien Enemy No. 10695
for Anna Maria Oldehaver

Your Certificate of Registration states that you were stout
black hair   brown eyes   born in Vava'u
with a distinctive scar on the back of your right hand.

In a report by *The Aliens Authority* Mr F.L.G. West tells me
that you were of good   loyal   character   despite
your German heritage.

A dashing signature, with a bold   dark line   confirms
that the Under-Secretary for the Minister of Police, concurred.

How shall I honour you on ANZAC day?
You, who duly registered as an Alien Enemy in our midst.

With a poem I am compelled   to elevate your memory   lift it
higher than the brittle pock marks and rusty imprint of History's
wake   buried in the bowels of *Archives NZ*.

While in my dreams, I will remember you as the mysterious
heroine who   jumped ship, skipped Apia, headed for Auckland
flew the coop and made me proud
four generations later.

Kamapuaʻa

you offer him cream cheese
with your fishy-false-eyelashes and empty texts

tucking in a suggestive X
that hints @ your between-legs-lies

hmmm your #secretagenda discovered
whoops! undercover mission aborted

Obsidian Nights

In the City of Obsidian rats creep in and out
of twisted streets wrapped in *Light*.

Light penetrates the veins of butchered mountains
that sweat tears into *The Holy Jug*.

The Holy Jug strews life's shards into a gaping mouth
full of bile, spit and *Blood-Shot-Night-Vigils*.

Blood-Shot-Night-Vigils fill the void with sorrow
and a dash of fragile *Hope*.

Cultural Diplomacy

Canberra 2009 –

The dead lake wallows
in a socket of remorse
Australia's guts are full
of politicians preaching prejudice.

Matilda wants a fair go
Pauline Hanson stole
the mic, locked
up Dinkum.

Truth is waiting, inside.

Tonga 2011 –'

The fecund trench slurs
into a kava bowl
Tonga's fate is stacked
in favour of fishy fiends.

Heilala is sick of being friendly
Crustaceous nodules bursting
with septic-sepia, flushed
out 'Ofa.

Love is waiting, outside.

Hawai'i 2013 –

The defiant mountain speaks
in tongues of fire
Hawai'i broke bread
with rapturous rats on a mission.

Aloha is sick of pineapples
Mr Dole devoured the food
chain, imprisoned
Her Majesty.

The planters sugar-coated Faith
then ate her, alive.

Honolulu's Homeless Live in Tents

```
           Honolulu's
            homeless
         live    in    tents
          sidewalk    squatting
           they                    wait
         watching                singing
          sighing                laughing
        cussing          `        crying
       their lives    away…with   the tide
```

One News

Auckland teens living in tents
at the back of New Lynn
shock   horror
as if this is new?

if the answer lies
in the question then the question
is who does this shock?

this reality was *voted* in

in a country where milk flows
down polluted rivers
where nest-egg-houses
are rotting
money buys You
a good education

We are beginning
to realise
investments
We didn't bank on.

The Fourth Labour Government
came and went
along with the 20th century
created a yawning   gap
for the primary opponent
to dominate
the match: 9-0
a generation-later

I look at our children
playing in the make-shift tent
we've pitched in our rented yard
and think:

if the question lies
in the answer then the answer
is home.

Whau Avondale

E hoa! we dive into electric currents
where salmon heads bob in boiling bliss
with photogenic grace
into a creamy coconut craze
of constellate proportions

piecemeal packages of tacky toast
litter lives full of spicy nights
hot green tea leaves
that fall from Uranus
under duvet covers

filled with jam
packed into suitcases
heading for the Kingdom
via Burger King
where disciples congregate

to break bread, drink milo
before saluting the magic carpet
on its way to Samoa
to get a DOPE haircut
like candy floss

cause I'm a *fia poto*
who rides the Oriental Express
on a super-ultra-sonic-spree
in the Maketi Whau

mining your mind
as you load up your truck
with socks stuffed with peas
on a deep-sea voyage
to get some kai
to put on ice

as we steam up *Club Raro*
for we are the victors
Aotearoa Warriors
the ones who fight
for tomorrow's hope

every moment, every day
with every breath
with all we've got
Left…because we must

protect our taonga
for to not do so is to be dust
and to be dust is to be dead
and dying is not an option, for us, today.

Wairaka

your shadow fell on my life
long before I knew your name
tussled and worn, your strength
arrived in parceled fragments
through cracked floorboards
lace curtains, polished doors

they tried to break you, leveled
your belly with tennis courts
gouged out your cheeks
- filled them in with chlorine
flipped you sunny-side-up
renamed you 'Albert'

while on your backside
they played Pepper-Pot
with your people's lives
chucked the children into a 'home'
aka: State-Care: straight-from-hell
then asked why they weren't behaving
like they 'ought to'…

every time you weep
for your blood brothers
Maugakiekie, Maungawhau
I feel you; every time you
call to Rangitoto, I hear you

and when it is no longer
bearable, I make the journey
to Muriwai, to bathe wounds
old and new, search for solace
safe-passage and permission
to let go of the need to harbour
pain, in exchange for peace…

Broken Waters

Birth

Kahlei came out
like a flying fish
burst my waters
so quickly
the midwife dropped
her net.

Sucking her thumb
Kahlei made me   whole.

Luka came out
like a shrieking shark
burst my waters
so quickly
the midwife screamed
louder than me.

Clutching his heart
Luka ripped me   in two.

D is for (Post-Natal) Depression
for all the mothers who can relate

Fluoxetine comes to visit
every morning
sits in my kitchen

taunts me
begs me
to swallow.

We've tried breaking up
said good-bye
countless times

withdrawn
recovered
withdrawn

held each other close
as we try to stitch my life
back together, again.

Shopping

Bread
Baby

Milk
Mastitis

Yoghurt
    Yo-Yo

Muesli
    Mad

Cheese
    Crackers

Washing Powder
      Will Power

Body Wash
    Wash Body

Wipes
    Wine

Nappies
Nap

Fruit
Cake

Baby Steps

Luka
is
l
e
a
r
n
i
n
g
how
to
walk
on
water
falls
abound
in his
dreams
I hover
unsure of my step
father's wrath in the wake of time

After Thought

You drop me a line on Facebook
hook
attached
no sinker.
You want to catch up
but only
after
your
trip.
I'm
g
u
t
t
e
d.

Post Natal

every time I give birth
there is a period
of silence
that follows my pain

months tumble
into years
poems percolate
milky waves

that keep current
affairs   at bay
until Tagaloa's tide
comes rushing in

flooding the two-year-mark
as the words start pouring out
of my baby's mouth

Ouch
for the Rt. Hon John Key

with a trolley full of grub
in the Pack n' Slave line
I read about a man
who pulled a pony's tail

          hard
          to read
          between
          the lines

but indications point
to the Act
being carried out
unlawfully

          without
          due consent
          consultation

or consideration
for animal rights
                                    it took place
                                    while this gentle man
          was ordering
          a latte
          on the fly   in Parnell

as I load up groceries
toddler on hip   daily paper   destroyed
a little hand yanks my head back   with a fistful
                                                         of hair

a thought pops out
someone really ought to tell that man
                              horsing around
                              hanky-panky

is a sure fire way
to get served

                              a caffeine kick
                              with a side of nuts

#SheepGate

Old McCully
had a Ministry
on Lambton Quay
he docked

some diplomats
on their way to Saudi
with Number 8 wire
to blood-let milk

on the front line
of His Dominion

Deference

Nod to leadership,
too easy to politic.
Live integrity.

After Life

on the way
to Eden
we   stop
to fish

for love ants
swimming
in a cup
of chicken

noodle soup
we bob
for sorrow
to bait

dreams bathing
in a riot
of wild
cocoa nimbi

we float
to pull
for light beetles
spinning

in a river
of funk, before
we drown out
the end.

Day Break

Tuli

your wings form a part of my body
delicate sinews woven into braided
flesh and bone

your plumage protects my spirit
soft feathers adorn memories
of 'ie-sina

you keep watch over me from above
at Tagaloa's side you sit
singing me home

Kindred
for Emmeline

our wings may be broken
but our hearts are in tact
we are keepers of the light
Dawn is coming

wings broken
hearts in tact
we keep the light
Dawn is coming

broken
hearts in tact
keep light
Dawn is coming

hearts
keep light
Dawn is coming

Dawn is coming
keep the light
in tact
our broken hearts
may be our wings

our broken hearts
may be our wings

www.ingramcontent.com/pod-product-compliance
Lightning Source LLC
Chambersburg PA
CBHW042333150426
43194CB00001B/38